D1326283

Search Party

George The Poet

Search Party

5 7 9 10 8 6 4

Virgin Books, an imprint of Ebury Publishing,
20 Vauxhall Bridge Road,
London SW1V 2SA

Virgin Books is part of the Penguin Random House group
of companies whose addresses can be found at
global.penguinrandomhouse.com

Copyright © George Mpanga 2015

George Mpanga has asserted his right to be identified as the
author of this Work in accordance with the Copyright,
Designs and Patents Act 1988

First published by Virgin Books in 2015

www.eburypublishing.co.uk

A CIP catalogue record for this book is available
from the British Library

ISBN 9780753556207

Penguin Random House is committed to a sustainable future for
our business, our readers and our planet. This book is made from
Forest Stewardship Council® certified paper.

Printed and bound in Great Britain by Clays Ltd, St Ives plc

This book is dedicated to our sister, Nabila Nanfuka.

You forced me to ask the important questions.

See you in a bit, angel.

Contents

III

Foreword

Island Records has a history of working with poets, most notably with Linton Kwesi Johnson, who released four albums on the label before setting up his own LKJ Records imprint through Island, and releasing records by Jamaican dub poet Mikey Smith.

When I first heard George it was one of those all too rare special moments. I knew instantly he *had* to be on Island. It was as if the baton was being passed. Not since Linton have I heard someone speak of the world we live in with such eloquence, intelligence, wit and directness. And for me, it's not about record sales or chart positions, it's about giving someone with so much important shit to say a platform upon which to say it.

In this ever hyper-stimulated world, with attention spans decreasing by the minute, George asks us to slow down, listen, understand and hopefully act accordingly. Important stuff … there's not much more important than that.

Darcus Beese, OBE
President, Island Records

Introduction

Although I studied politics for six years, I always felt alienated from it. Let me be clear: I wasn't uninterested, just alienated. Discussing politics always felt like critiquing a story that I actually wanted to co-write, so I would approach debates with an innate frustration, a predicated impatience, which I never acknowledged, much less understood. Over time, as I learned more about myself and the world around me, I realised why this was. I felt that these discussions were limited by the constructions and constrictions of the political arena – the things that we were encouraged to discuss and to ignore.

In a world of oversight, I felt invisible, as the many dimensions of my identity were so often disregarded in the context of 'important' debates. My environment, my musical taste, my displaced nationality, my experience of social mobility – all at a young age – were conspicuous by their absence in the mainstream media.

Transitioning from my estate to a selective grammar school added to the confusion. At school we were taught that there existed a Type, and this Type was somehow more deserving of the superior teaching and grooming that the institute offered. Although I loved learning, I resented this concept, not least because it flew in the face of everything I experienced in the place where I grew up. Throughout my teen years I developed navigation strategies for my different social settings. They would often entail altering my dialect, filtering my thoughts and translating my experiences. I suspect this is something most migrants will relate to; however, it's a bit weird when you've only ever lived in one country. I realised that I was part of a small section of society. My skin colour alone put me at under 3 per cent of the population. Confusingly for me, I was still 100 per cent black. Was I supposed to resign the remaining 97 per cent of my identity to the peripheries of the British experience?

Luckily, I'm stubborn. I was always adamant that my life was more valuable to the world than the Type that the school promoted. The Type was someone else's idea, but that person didn't know what I knew. They hadn't seen what I'd seen. Similarly, I rejected the Type that many of my friends back home had subscribed to. Some things never made sense to me and I hated pretending to conform. So I wrote rhymes. Sometimes they articulated my thoughts literally, sometimes implicitly. Sometimes they channelled my friends' experiences vicariously, but at *all* times, they told the truth. In all its subjectivity and its objectivity, the truth – can't believe I'm saying this – set me free.

To date, no one really knows anything about me other than the hard facts of my existence: where I'm from, what I do, etc. Some think I'm a poet because I can't rap. Some think I'm a naïve idealist. Some even think that I'm a well-meaning Cambridge graduate trying to compensate for my guilt about some privileged upbringing by telling other people's stories. Thanks to these poems, I'm clear that none of these perceptions matters. The truth doesn't care who finds it, who sees it or who shares it – it just shines, regardless.

I studied politics for six years, now I'm finally ready to start my Search Party.

I

St Raphael's Estate

I'm from Raph's,

Home of guns and staffs,

Shooters running up on dons in caffs.

In Year Six he was getting Level Ones in Maths,

A couple of grams later, he's better with numbers,

Getting a gun cos youngers are wetting up youngers;

Parents' debt is humongous;

Dead end wherever you run cos

Hunters are setting up stunters for stepping up funds

If they don't get enough punters.

We don't want to be those old men in the bookies

Betting our funds as drunkards;

Smoking like we're forgetting our lungs have fungus,

Watching the effects of poverty getting our youngers'

youngers.

Shots sound like fireworks when I wake up at night,

My mum's screaming out the window, trying to break

up a fight.

I don't know anyone who was born and raised here, spent

All their days here without no incidents;

So when I watch a child grow into this

I know it's not about coincidence. You go into this

Mad world with nothing but a phone in your hand –

Just a handheld – but no one's holding your hand.

You can read about the ghetto and watch the film *Roots*,

But you won't get it till you cotch with real youts,

Watch ghetto girls play hopscotch in little boots;

Even when the food ain't top-notch it still shoots,

So we chill on the blocks and build zoots.

Come to Raph's for guns and staffs,

A lot of homes are broken, a lot of sons are mad;

Every other kid that becomes a shotter wants a dad.

You wouldn't believe the pressure a lot of youngsters had.

The grass is always greener, but not amongst the sad.

They say the apple never falls far from the tree,

But isn't it called 'rotten' once it's bad?

You won't understand me if you don't know Raph's –

Crackheads, prostitutes and sociopaths.

You can't avoid offending the hotheads.

Shit schools defending their Ofsteds.

Four faces you've never seen before

Watching everyone who looks seventeen or more

From a tinted car, pretending they're not Feds.

Essential services that haven't got a budget.

You try and rise above it,

But everything around you says

'You're not above it' – you gotta love it.

The Set-up

They grabbed me from behind and threw me against
    the wall.
My temper flared – I assumed we were meant to brawl,
Until they turned me around and I saw the uniform.
Aren't you the law? I wish I knew before.
One of them said something about resisting arrest
And I swear down my heart became a fist in my chest.
This kid's fifteen.

Does he really deserve this lack of respect
As you scream profanities at the back if his neck?
He surprises himself with the tears in his eyes,
The confusion and shock that he hears in his cries.
As he fights to reclaim his masculinity,
His angry responses are fears in disguise.

That's when I felt the hate and fire enter me.

Is this the fate that I'm meant to see?

Then the pagans tried attentively,

Attempting to plea for peace: mistaken identity.

I told you that in a minute, only five have passed

And I've seen four people I know slowly driving past.

They get no explanation,

Just an image that matches their whole expectation.

I heard one mumble, 'How do we manage this one?'

You can start by fucking off, the damage is done.

I told myself no matter what challenges come

This place won't beat me, it's a scavenger's slum.

Why's everyone acting like savages, Mum?

One minute some kid was having his fun,

The next minute this kid's been stabbed in his lung,

Now to retaliate someone's grabbing his gun.

And amidst all of this, I fit a description.

At the time I was too indignant to listen,

But I can't say the police took a malignant position.

How am I supposed to win living so close to sin?

Got to think out the box with the walls closing in,

So I work at the barber's to make a little dough.

The money's slow, but where else can I go?

I'm underage. Plus I'm still in this 'younger' stage.

I'm a target for some little villain that's on a rage,

And I don't wanna end up a still on a front page.

I don't want to be around people I don't like

And people that don't like me deep in the road life.

It's a secret my parents have been keeping my whole life:

The whole thing is a set-up.

That wasn't my last mix-up with sinful banditry.

I started to see this kind of thing more standardly.

That's why I believe that a simple plan from me

Could turn this whole thing around single-handedly.

The elders say the ends used to be decent,

And all this madness is unusually recent,

But it's a problem that Culture can be used to defeat and

The bottom line is I refuse to be beaten.

Ride Out

The only way he can overcome the hopelessness that claimed everyone around him is by embracing the likelihoods of death and incarceration. Only then can he be the architect of his own destiny. So he hurtles mindlessly towards his mid-twenties, energised by the prospect of autonomy in a world of constrictions.

Maybe if he wasn't so preoccupied with survival, he'd be in search of purpose. But that's like trying to build on water; he's better off riding the wave.

His Mistakes

Every mood swing was a different mask that he'd worn
As protection. You treat him like he asked to be born.
But you're the one that finds it hard to be warm.
He tries his best not to cause you any trouble, but
You never hesitate to rock his boat.
Slap him in the face because he forgot his coat.
Let's be honest, though, you know it's not his fault.
It's not about discipline; sister, you're stressed.
You're mad at your worst and you're pissed at your best.
You've contemplated opening your wrist and your chest
Is heavy; you don't have someone to talk to.
It's all bottled up, because once you've undone the
    corkscrew
You won't gain a thing from some dumb support group;
And your son doesn't understand what a piss this takes,

18

So he pays a heavy price for his mistakes.

So heavy each shoulder's numb.

He knows it's dumb, but for your sake he holds his tongue

And holds a grudge. He holds it within

With no release, until he's old enough to go to the gym.

I know it's not my business, babes.

But can we have a quick word, just as mates?

Given that some of the fault is this estate's,

Should he really have to pay for his mistakes?

•

She has a volatile temperament,

So she tends to vent until her temper's spent.

And she doesn't notice the efforts you make,

Even when you give a hundred and ten per cent.

Sometimes you catch her looking at you funny.

Sunshine doesn't even seem too sunny,

Because instead of enjoying a cool breeze,

She'd rather moan and complain about your school fees.

Like you asked to be born.

Like you're a bad spirit given the chance to reform in

    this bastardly form.

Like you're the one that found it hard to be warm.

Like we can trade-in the cards that we've drawn.

Like you enjoyed all the times you annoyed her.

Like you exploit her like the guy who employs her.

Like you like having to dodge and avoid her.

Like you like looking like the man who destroyed her.

It wasn't your fault. But please don't resent her

For rocking your boat just because of your coat.

Just like you, she didn't get a say,

She doesn't know why there couldn't be a better way.

She wants to see her son shine, but all predictions

Of the weather say tomorrow's gonna be a wetter day.

Looking at the payslip numbers you can't tell,

But back in the day your mum was a smart girl.

She just never has any money for Christmas breaks,

Because she spent it all paying for his mistakes.

She singlehandedly raised you –

For that alone there's a lot of praise due.

As for him, you can't pretend you don't fantasise,

But his identity's something you can romanticise,

Even though you're a child he was scared to claim.

She's the only one there to blame.

But you have your own mistakes to make.

Don't repeat theirs – learn to bear the pain.

She's invested everything she's got in you,

So think of these investments as business stakes.

A parent's shortcomings aren't a kid's disgrace.

You're just man enough to cover his mistakes.

He second-guessed his worth.

That's an error that many beginners make.

But even though you were an accident,

You weren't necessarily a mistake.

Payday

A generation came of age in the financial crisis,
But what does this mean in real time?
What's the state of play for the day-to-day?
What do they eat at mealtimes?
Maybe they feel fine.

Through record numbers of youth unemployment,
I walked alongside four young lives in Croydon –
A borough that's economically divided:
Some save, some rave, some can only wonder
If tomorrow comes what's gonna be provided?
'Then again,' they say, 'as long as we've survived it.'

Some lessons can only be learned, they can't
    be taught.

Some fights were lost no matter how hard we fought.

No matter where the camera goes, some scenes can't

be caught

And no matter how much we make, some dreams

can't be bought.

There are those who would say this is art.

Budgeting, bargaining … business smart.

Hustling's for hustlers, 'change' is up for grabs,

Therefore becoming accustomed is for customers.

Others would say contentment starts within.

With hard living you can't give in,

Not least in front of a rival, you need something to

fight for.

There's no choice but to hunt for survival.

II

My City

My city has a lot of faces.

Some can be found in forgotten places.

Comfortably sound with a lot of graces.

The sun could be down on his hungry town,

But in London he found him a shot at greatness.

My city has a lot of faces.

Some can tell you what a 'loss of faith' is.

Before we hated people we were all created equal,

Then we learnt to despise the strife and we forgot variety's

The spice of life – look around you.

Constantly standing on the brink of history,

Watching newsreaders linking mystery,

Even though a few reporters taught us to be cautious,

    cos they

Stink of this disease called inconsistency, see

My city has a lot of faces.

Four of them belonging to Big Ben, the rest of them,

Hidden behind big business and Big Brother,

Ensures all of them are monitored with them.

Under social tensions you can see London languishes:

Thirty per cent minorities, three hundred languages.

Differences – race and class – it's all enormous,

But the common ground we found surpasses all the borders.

It's funny how Londoners are from time to time:

Only got the time to grind and whine.

Technically, I'm from an elegant city,

But I'm not the kind to wine and dine;

I grew up around lots of crime, the violent kind.

You might have heard about the rocks, the grime, the hype
  and shine.

It's not just Cockney rhyming slang,

We've got block-beef, violent gangs,

Awkward interactions which most don't force,

Children navigating through postcode wars

In estates with the least funding –

Look at the state of east London.

That's a paradox: witness economy blooming

For the have-a-lots business is gonna be booming,

But there's a difference between having a front-row seat

And watching from the sidelines.

TFL knows the world is your Oyster,

As long as you can afford it,

Even though you might need to remortgage

Just to get from Aldwych to Shoreditch.

Inconvenient if you're poor, which

Could be expected in a tax system where the more rich get
more rich.

Two hundred and seventy-three times the wealth of the
poorest …

Yet your door is next door to the extra poor.

We look on the bright side, but we're vexed for sure,

Like all we have to ourselves is sex and war,

And a lotta diversity –

So what could I personally hate a complexion for?

I see different coloured hands outstretched for more.

Feel free to come to London

And still see the London Dungeon.

Experience a Tube of mad claustrophobics,

Where food and bad posture don't mix,

And join us in moving along to the groove of the song.

What a sight to see – we could swap a nicety.

Some of us feel you've forgotten my city,

But hopefully you'll be proving us wrong.

If you can take the rough with the smooth, then it's on.

How Does It Feel?

How does it feel to be misperceived?

Does it justify the urge to disbelieve?

Cos when you disbelieve you don't have to expect,

Which can help you accept what you have to accept.

Through disbelief you avoid disappointments

And disappointments hurt, so you enjoy this
avoidance.

All you have left is 'I told you so', by which

Time the relevance is as void as the point is.

You're resistant to being pissed on for good

If you own the extent to which you're misunderstood.

So how does it feel to be misperceived?

It doesn't feel like anything if you disbelieve.

That doesn't sound very appealing, though;

At the end of the day where does the feeling go?

Oh yeah. You don't care.

You've trained yourself not to go there.

Cos you felt like you can't change your world,

So instead you trained yourself to change yourself.

Hopefully you can benefit from the changes.

It's actually quite clever, but it's dangerous.

Because insecurity isn't necessarily immaturity –

It's arguably the essence of your inner purity.

Think about it.

Everything your heart has invested

Must be at least in part manifested

In the stack of the crap you bear off the back of the

    fact you care.

In fact, who cares?

Clearly, within we're just conforming.

We're not really living, we're just performing.

Two notions we invent: 'pride' and 'hope', but

In reality, all of us consent by default, cos there's

Strength in numbers and this immunity's fine.

It's just why I can't pretend that this community's mine.

I'm not at the forefront of this community's mind,

Which is truthfully fine,

As long as you don't feed me this 'community' line!

Just consider this:

My life could have been yours, with a twist.

Monsters

When I was a kid

My biggest fear was nightmares.

Now I fear daydreams.

I'd rather have monsters under my bed than

    skeletons in my closet.

Rice and Peas

Easy. Nice and easy.

Oxtail, plantain and rice and peas, please.

Yeah, yeah, yeah, 'plantin' / 'plantain',

Either way it's a word dark skin can't claim.

Imagining my father – him and his wife –

Escaping Uganda's imminent strife

In the Eighties; packing up his bags, booking a flight

And embarking on an immigrant life.

And so the story's written in Falkland-glory-smitten,

Broken Tory Britain.

Sorting out the housing situation

On an estate with thousands of Jamaicans,

With a brand new set of trials and tribulations.

I eventually ventured out into the Asian suburbs.

Started to wonder why the ends was called the inner city.

It wasn't a place of major commerce.

My elder said the area used to be white.

I've never seen a picture, but he's usually right.

Maybe parents feared for their kids and hurried

them out …

Is this what all those anti-immigration people are

worried about?

Losing this? To people who are overqualified and

underpaid?

We're the ones afraid.

Because, if the social mobility focus is now gone,

Then Progress is something we're both missing out on.

The Lazy Dog

Imagine having a starving hound

Barking loud without calming down.

You know the reason for the dog's bad mood:

It's been a while since the dog's had food.

But the sound is more annoying than Crazy Frog.

What's his problem? Must be a lazy dog.

Skulking around trying to act hard,

When there's more than enough to eat in the backyard.

You don't take him running, cos you go to jog alone,

But just before you leave you throw the dog a bone,

Thinking: 'He looks depressed, but he won't faze me.

If he's that hungry he shouldn't be so lazy.'

You don't call the dog by name, cos he responds to 'Oi!'

Sees the meat on the bone and jumps for joy,

But it's out of his reach, cos he's tied to the kennel

And he can't exactly hitch a ride in a Renault.

It doesn't take a dissertation with Harvard references

To work out the dog's gonna starve to death because

Every time you throw him something to eat

It lands metres in front of his feet.

But you leave the house, you go on a run and huff, puff,

And get so distracted you think you've done enough stuff

To provide; this is food you're too kind to retract.

Blind to the fact that he's tied to the back.

See, to give someone a chance …

Isn't the same as to set them free.

That's why when someone's in trouble …

It's not enough to just let them be.

All you can see is the fact that he sells crack,

Ignoring the fact that he's actively held back.

He's actually, well, trapped. That's why he traps.

But it's much bigger than him. That's why he raps.

What's the point in claiming to sing a song of hope

When passing judgement? How's a sinner gonna cope?

We're planning a prison break – bring along a rope

And if the rope ain't long enough, bring a longer rope.

Suppliers give the buyers, give the slinger stronger dope.

And the heart tells the head that ignorance is bliss,

But the joint can't work if the ligaments are twisted.

I hope you understand the significance of this.

There's so much potential for magnificence at risk,

But just like my words the iterance persists,

Just like my words the iterance persists …

I hope you can see what belligerence this is.

Believer

She's a good actress, knows how to spin a web.

You call her Sigourney Weaver.

You don't know her body like you used to.

And she doesn't make you horny, either.

You love her more than you like her,

Cos you think she's a bit of a diva.

She loves you more than she likes you,

Cos you're a bit of an underachiever.

She used to be someone you had a cool time with,

Now you just think she's small-minded,

Laughing at the dreams you're grafting at, it seems

She thinks you're short-sighted or blinded.

But she's worked too hard to leave you

And you're too indecisive to leave her.

So all your expectations and hopes,

Just disappear into the ether.

Life is suffocating you and a spliff is the

Only time you get a breather.

But you always look forward to Monday,

Cos on Sunday, you're a believer.

You wish he would treat you different.

He can be insensitive, and when

You're at your lowest, he's Peter Griffin.

He always wants support that you can't give him.

You laugh at him more than you laugh with him.

And you wouldn't know what to do if he proposed;

You could be setting yourself up to be an ex-wife.

Then having to wait until the next life

Before you even see the ghost of your sex life.

Makes you want to kill what's left of his sex drive,

Even though the only 'body' he's remotely

    interested in

Is the one on that stupid X5 or S-Type

Or whatever he's always banging on about.

You're hanging on without being showered

    with love

And the powers above know you were never

    planning on a drought,

But life is so dry …

And a drink is the only time you get a breather.

You always look forward to Monday, though,

Cos on Sunday, you're a believer.

Please Doubt Me

'Good GCSEs, George, you smashed your
    performance!'
Same year I got my national insurance,
Got myself a job, carried on studying,
I just might be a person of actual importance,
From a place where no one seems to matter.
One way or another most of the dreams just shatter.
But everywhere I go in the place I call my ends
I see support and a smiling face on all my friends,
So why is the school telling me I can't go to
    Cambridge?
I think they got the game wrong; so far I've won.
Do they know where I came from? How far I've come?
I won't make this about me and them,
I'll just ask the world to doubt me again.

Planning Permission

Life is four things at any one time:

A decision and a reaction in the heart and the mind.

So I asked God why the scars that He heals

Are always paper cuts from the cards that He deals.

He said, 'In this life a man either builds or destroys.

No planning permission. You plan by your

    permission.

So keep your hand by your munitions,

And stand by your decisions.'

The Spectrum

My perception of colour can be altered by

A simple adjustment to my eyes.

Therefore navy blue could be baby blue,

So why do we treat colour the way we do?

We don't know what an objective perception is,

Because we can't overcome how subjective the

spectrum is.

Life is a collage of views you perceive,

And that preconditions what you choose to believe,

So if navy blue could be baby blue,

The problem or the solution may be you.

Allow me to explain.

All we really have is the perceptible, the tangible,

And, of course, the ability to understand it all.

So why do humans act so strange

In a world full of facts, when the facts don't change?

You'd think we could at least agree on what's not fair

And distinguish between validity and hot air,

Because you believe in the ability of humankind

To figure out anything, given enough room

    and time.

And across the board that affects how you perform;

It's the reason why when in doubt you conform.

Cos you feel like collectively we have enough

    intelligence

To pursue what we want, and we want what's best.

Therefore, a social democratic agenda

Constantly presents us with new prospects.

So what's next?

Sit around and wait for the change to come?

That might seem a little strange to some,

Because according to the facts the change

    is overdue,

It's just something that many of us don't pursue.

Cos we believe in the natural order of things,

There's no parallel universe or Lord of the Rings;

There's only one predictable, logical existence

And any alternative claim warrants your resistance.

But the inconvenient truth … is that reality

Is arbitrary.

We share the gift of life, the gift of boys, the gift

    of girls,

We share the same planet, but live in different worlds.

Numbers don't lie, they show great precision,

But at the end of the day they don't make decisions:

People call the shots. Or not.

We spend so much time discerning the fine line between

Picking our battles and turning a blind eye,

That we forget we're in this together.

If we win this war we win this forever.

I'd love to paint a rainbow of cordiality,

But I'm going to have to interrupt your reality.

We can't chase the secrets of truth and enjoyment

When we're facing record numbers of youth

    unemployment

In a world where 'unemployed' translates to 'null
and void'.
Jobs require competence, this doesn't inspire
confidence.

One in four kids is BME in primary school.
That's when life's about PS3 and trying to be cool.
That figure slips to one in five in secondary school –
If we assume meritocracy that's a necessary fall.
An eighth of the workplace is from a minority
ethnic background –
They're represented by one sixteenth of the
boardroom.
So what do we make of the facts now?

Different people have different skill sets:
If society doesn't value what they can trade
The implication is they just do not make the grade.
But it's not like the talent and the spirit isn't there;
We need to actively make this pyramid a square.
In the last three years the rate of unemployment
Among young black males has more than doubled.

It's easy to look at a group and call them troubled,

But nothing is isolated – we're all in trouble.

A more representative workforce means better

Understanding and hence customer satisfaction,

So let's strategise and adjust to the plan of action;

With the right managers the game could become equal,

So let's give a platform to capable young people.

How long this will take is hard to say,

But everybody's got a part to play.

All I ask is you allow yourself to be bothered

Every morning when you start the day.

Your approach to recruitment, your involvement

   of students –

Challenge your thought process to support progress.

This summer we turned to the Games for proper unity,

Now let's go for gold in the race for opportunity,

Because after the ceremonies, the fire and celebration,

We still need to inspire a generation.

The Feeling's Mutual

We're in the same boat.

The dream we were sold as kids isn't impossible; it's
just unlikely.

I'm chasing my destiny, while evading commitment.

You're drifting towards loneliness and further away
from fertility.

Who needs trust when you've got mutual interests?

Full-time

Love is a full-time job.

It doesn't start at nine and finish at five.

It will either spark your fire or diminish your drive.

There are no days off.

There are no ways of making sure it pays off.

There's no protection from redundancy.

There's no guarantee of loyalty from the company.

Cos when you give someone your soul,

You're a sole trader.

And when you think with your heart –

That's a no-brainer.

One Number

Do you know what I hate more than waking up?

Waking up without you.

Lying there trying to write scripts and stories,

I just end up making stuff about you.

It's like the universe thinks it's been too good to me:

'We gave him her, let's make him suffer now, too.'

But it can't undo the effects of the good habits

That I'm taking up around you.

Your love is sound and your love's profound, too.

So I'll be picking you up around two?

All I want is you inside of my room.

One is two divided by two,

But two's still one number,

Two's just one number.

One plus one is a slightly bigger one …

Do you see what I see with the sum?

Don't I get along so nicely with your mum?

I can't wait until we move into a slightly bigger drum.

Your body language is my mother tongue.

If there's more women like you, then I've got to find
my brothers some.

But we both know that's impossible,

Because you're The One and I'm The Other One.

All I want is you inside of my room.

One is two divided by two,

But two's still one number,

Two's just one number.

The Ends of the Earth

A child is not a portion of an adult.

It's not a partial being.

A child is an absolute person,

An entire life.

The fact that the child is developing,

Doesn't mean it's incomplete.

This just makes it especially important for the

Child to drink and eat, and get a decent wink

   of sleep.

Many children are given less than children deserve;

Such is the world they entered at birth.

But all it takes is one friend … one friend

Who's willing to go to the ends of the earth.

For children in the hardest circumstances,

A friend who gives in to no resistance.

Whether down the road or around the globe,

One who's prepared to go the distance,

One who's not scared to show persistence.

No task is too tall, no ask is too small

To send through ... to attend to.

You could be a friend, too.

Go to the ends of the Earth, for children.

Scapegoat

At any given point life is as complicated as it ever

   has been

And as simple as it will ever be,

Hence my preoccupation with legacy.

I think life wanted to show me its potential …

And you are the window that it revealed it through.

That's why I'm not scared to build with you.

There's no denying, no matter what I feel.

The situation we're in is not ideal,

But I'm gonna ride still.

My sanity depends on my family and friends;

The same family and friends to whom my salary extends;

The same family and friends that give me clarity and sense

At times when life is apparently intense.

To everyone else I'm just a real good actor,

But you are my feel-good factor.

There's no problem I can't dissolve,

No situation I can't resolve,

When I keep you in mind, heart and soul.

You're the reason I dare to believe.

You're the reason I'm not scared to achieve,

I'm prepared to give whatever you're prepared to receive.

You are my scapegoat.

In the Quiet

I'm tryna take it all in, remember that I'm lucky

To be awake this morning;

Start rapping without a beat and before you know it

They start clapping and shouting and call you poet …

All cos God blessed my ability to record flows on a sheet.

I'm the only poet that's all over the street.

I used to think success was having more shows in a week,

But what does that matter if doors close when I speak?

Ask anyone, I used to go church.

Now there's no guide to how I choose to soul-search.

But you're smarter than you give yourself credit for.

You're incredible – I'm sorry I never said it more.

I propose a clean slate.

I just wanna raise the ghetto like Green Gate.

Too many kids have seen hate

And out here bids just seem great,

So I'm tryna save him from prison food,

But he thinks he's weak if he isn't rude.

Then his older came up to me like 'Yo big man. I'm a
   big fan.

You got the sense that I want for my kid fam.'

I said a blessing ain't a blessing unless I can

Share it with man.

But then again ... I spread myself too thin.

Why should I drown tryna help you swim?

Come to the table with two long hands,

But I really wanna know what else you bring.

For a kid with no money the appeal is great.

What you think he knows about property and real estate?

He thinks his weapon is something he can't do without
   at all,

But if I'm not careful he won't talk to me about it all.

So I gotta give him the message, but make it palpable.

Cos he thinks I've never been broke. Never been angry.

I need to make the medicine candy.

You don't have to be a conscious yout to contribute.

III

Passion Fruit

My city has a lot of faces.

It's a place where self-pity hasn't got a basis.

Innovation doesn't come at a decent price,

But look hard enough and you'll be surprised.

On a council estate you'd think

Every other person has a mouthful of hate.

And we never really learn how to debate,

We just shout to relate or have a bout with a mate.

But we embrace misconceptions,

We don't make excuses, knowing

Adversity gets the creative juices flowing.

When the local area's the target space

We can separate the art from the marketplace

And keep it pure. Premature.

Like nothing that you have seen before.

Some of us have been on an uncharted journey.

To all the latecomers this one started early.

Out of our crazy location

Came the wonder of the pirate radio station.

Jungle became Garage and Garage became Grime,

Married to the streets, how did this marriage
remain fine?

We were forced to manage and tame crime,

Challenged to aim high and balance the game right.

And we were allowed to be mad at the same time.

We just said how we were feeling and it became
rhyme.

We definitely deserve every blessing that we have
earned,

But there's still a bigger lesson that we have learned:

No matter how difficult the game,

You can always rise to critical acclaim.

This place raised me, so I stick to what I know,

And that's exactly why you can picture what I flow.

When you're in the paradox of a fiery storm,

Paralysed in a place that parasites entirely swarmed,

Think about the heat it takes for iron to be warmed,
Think about the pressure required for diamond to
be formed.
We're the lucky ones … we're the lucky ones.
Cos when you can't get involved
Consumerism and fashion is brutal.
You might start to doubt whether ration is truthful.
But life is sweet when your passion is fruitful.

Different countries and different colours, sisters
and brothers
Given to mothers, significant others,
From the butcher to the baker that baked the
pancake,
Gimme a handshake: you helped shape the
landscape,
Even if you think you didn't play a major part,
Even if you had a change of heart,
You touched my life because you played your part.
You changed my world when you played your part.
All we had was art and self-belief.
Before all of this we never felt relief.

And that initially affected the image that we
     projected,
From how we handled difference to how we dealt
     with beef.
We're the lucky ones. Yeah, we're the lucky ones.

My city has a lot of faces.
It's a place where sunny days start off cold.
My city has a lot of races:
It's a treasure chest with a heart of gold.

Take heed. Take heart.
Take hold of my hand and we'll take over the land,
Assist me in taking a hold … of making
History and breaking the mould.

Life on Earth

I don't know about them, but I'm really out here.

I see what poverty does.

They're asking if it bothers me, cos.

I can say anything I like right now

And I'm saying this, so it obviously does.

Change isn't something coming for you;

Change is something you do.

Spend a month in the shoes

Of somebody that can't run from the news,

Someone that doesn't have something to lose,

Somewhere you don't have the comfort to cruise

And see what can come from the blues.

She can't protect her son from the crews,

He can't protect his mum from a bruise –

And you're not expecting someone to lose?

You're not expecting someone to lose?

What would you do if you grew up in a house full

of love,

In a hood full of hate,

With immigrant parents and a media culture

That never really understood your estate?

They don't like none of us.

Don't even know no one like none of us.

They think we're scrappy and dread.

We think we're happy. Instead

It's a bit of both. But with that being said,

You could lose your life on the bus.

You could lose your sanity, temper,

Funding for your family centre;

You could lose a family member.

The good news is you can at least vent stuff.

The bad news is all the good news is apparently

spent up.

It's like the prayers haven't been sent up.

The only thing left to lose … is control of the anger

we've pent up.

But you won't lose. Will you?

You won't lose. Will you?

Look at me. Will you?

I didn't think so.

Life on Mars

I believe we're stronger than we think.

I believe we can last much longer than we think.

I believe in me. I believe in you.

I believe pain is just weakness leaving you.

This life can be a roundabout,

That's why you're down and out.

You hear voices and want to drown them out.

Whenever you find something to smile about,

You find something else to frown about.

So the sound of doubt's much louder now.

Gone are the days when you could clown around, too.

Cos you can't escape this cloud around you.

You're clearly strained, you look really drained;

You feel like no one else knows your pain

And you can't stand what controls your brain,

But I can only tell cos I feel the same.

I deal with pain. I get disappointed and think

'Why fill your brain with ideals again?'

But you know what? That's part of the struggle.

And as things get harder to juggle,

I realise that we're made for this.

Whether you're religious or atheist,

To exist is to fight. The ability to fight?

That's what safety is.

I don't know much.

I don't know if there's life on Mars.

But where I'm from, we fight for ours,

Ride for ours, die for ours.

You'll be fine, you know.

You could've given up a long time ago,

But you're still here. That's a sign of hope.

Everybody's out here trying to cope.

Maybe the Martians have it all figured out,

Laughing at whatever we're talking about.

Maybe it's a front with magnificent PR

So we can't see how insignificant we are.

Cash and status might be a massive waste

And if that's the case, we're likely to trash this place,

But who cares? We're here now.

Life's hard. Swear down.

You've got to learn to fight, I don't care how.

It's gonna be all right, just let your tears out.

Accept your fears now, let's get prepared now.

I'm not scared. Are you scared?

Through your weakest sobs you can speak to gods

And I bet you any money you can beat the odds,

So don't let them take the life out of you.

No matter what you're up against, I'm down for you.

See, I don't know much.

I don't know if there's life on Mars.

But where I'm from, we fight for ours,

Ride for ours, die for ours.

You'll be fine, you know.

You could've given up a long time ago,

But you're still here. That's a sign of hope

Everybody's out here trying to cope.

The Way I Am

You don't resent the sun for shining at noon;

It wouldn't be right to assume it's undermining

the moon.

You don't resent the tide for climbing the land;

You understand that it's not undermining

the sand.

You don't challenge the boundlessness of your

mind span

You don't ask a penguin or an ostrich why it can't

fly, but time can.

Your lungs can understand a breeze that breathes

over trees and leaves

Whenever it decides to pass by the scene.

You don't ask the grass why it's green.

You don't question how fast life has been.

These things are as natural as the things that

make a man.

So you can understand why I am the way I am.

Go Home

I wonder how much compassion you'll hear

In a country where the leaders spread irrational fear?

It's discouraging, if not depressing to learn

That a witch-hunt is now our most pressing concern.

To keep those Johnnies on their feet,

Stations need Boarder Agency bobbies on the beat.

Be sure and make the scene loud and clear …

Because they should be out of here.

'GO HOME' all over lorries on the street?

That's the government's best suggestion?

Well, such a subversive approach must be

Entirely necessary. Which begs the question:

How many illegal immigrants are there in this

country?

Oh, you don't quite know? So how can you justify

The psychological impact of this whole sideshow?

Like race relations' disintegration,

This is either oversight or misinformation.

But control's about taking sides,

So it's no surprise you plan to roll this out

    nationwide.

'GO HOME' harks back to a miserable memory

Of hatred towards an invisible enemy,

And it's wrong of government to use this phrase.

It's wrong of government to abuse its place,

Because language is a gateway to an attitude –

That is menacing, that is hostile, and that is rude.

In using those words you validate the behaviour

    that comes with them.

And in doing so, you appropriate the bigot that

    runs with them.

This is kiddish, it's foolish, it's not British – it's

    brutish.

No one in the country knows how many illegal

    immigrants there are.

Ninety-four per cent of the population know

That a lot of illegal immigrants don't look like them.

If government can't be bothered to tread carefully,

   why should anyone else?

My Mandela

You were born alone.

Then from your innocence you were torn and

   thrown

Into the unjust world that you inherited.

But where your heart is, that's where you call

   a home.

In the midst of a violent era

You have the nerve to defy the terror

And fight the better fight.

We have a right to get it right,

Cos life shouldn't depend on trial and error.

Nor should it depend on the ruthless clashing,

Claiming generations of youth assassins.

They all can talk and say you ought to walk away,

But 'struggle' is just the name for fruitless passion.

You can picture how the world could potentially be,

And believe that's a day you'll eventually see,

Or you can accept the unacceptable:

Not expect it all to change and pretend to be free.

What to do? Do you fold?

Do you back down, do as you're told?

Fade to the background in the face of a crackdown

Aimed at you and your own?

Twenty-seven years is a long time to hope.

Twenty-seven years is a long time to pray.

Twenty-seven years is twenty-seven reasons for

Me to stand here with a strong mind today,

Because I can't claim to have faith

If I only believe when it's safe.

You lost everything, everything but the will to live,

The will to persevere and still forgive.

Sometimes I wonder if they knew they were wrong.

You weren't a convict, but you were convicted.

Sometimes I wonder if you knew all along,

Cos even in conflict you weren't conflicted.

Just like me, you were born alone,

But what you did for the place that you called a home

Laid foundations for the future:

You were the rock that became a cornerstone.

In the midst of a violent era

The hardest thing is to defy the terror.

But life shouldn't depend on trial and error.

Goodbye, Mandela.

My Mandela.

Leaders of the New School

Change isn't just coming for you;

Change is something you do.

These are the moments you'll never see again.

This is the youngest you'll ever be again.

Once these times have come and gone,

All you'll have left is the memory of them.

Life is a moment.

The story doesn't need the writer's involvement.

So edit this for me. Don't embellish and twist it, please.

Don't embed it in mystery.

You know your credit in history

Amounts to more than your credit history.

Edit this for me.

When I leave this world I take my ideas to the
    graveyard, too.
'Impossible' is just a word people use to describe
    something they can't do.
Impossible is spending twenty-seven years in prison
And still coming out with the clearest vision.
Impossible is the life of Nelson Mandela.
But the world doesn't need another Nelson Mandela.
The world needs you …
The best version of yourself that you have to offer.
And if the world isn't ready for you
You've got to give it to them good and proper.

These are the moments you'll never see again.
This is the youngest you'll ever be again.
Once these times have come and gone,
All you'll have left is the memory of them.

We are the leaders of the New School
And we'd like to welcome to the class new students.
Starting from the bottom is an uphill struggle,
But that's the nature of a grassroots movement.

We are the leaders of the New School.

I don't know about you, but I'm prepared to reign.

I'm not crazy, they're deranged

If they think we're old enough to be scared of change.

School Blues

Children from disadvantaged backgrounds start
Secondary school with lower literacy skills than
    their peers.
The reality of disparity is revealed in their years.
By the third Key Stage at Year Seven
They're seventeen per cent worse off – that's at the
    age of eleven.

It's time to stage an intervention –
One that's designed for engaging their attention.
Music has the ability to speak from the heart,
So kids often admire those at the peak of the art.
See, education and art go hand in hand;
There is no reason to keep them apart.

We need a system that marries the two,

And most classrooms haven't found the balance.

But what if we engaged students with people they

Celebrate for the most profound of talents?

What if schools made use of musicians

As a means of getting their students to listen?

Analysis and discussion of actual lyrics

Helps learning to occur in more natural spirits.

I've done the same thing myself with poetry.

It doesn't just sow a seed, it helps to grow a tree.

For Stephen

In 1993 a knife cut through a family,

Separating father and son, mother and child.

Following this tragedy was the open friction caused by

No convictions in the subsequent trial.

Stephen Lawrence was eighteen at the time of the attack.

His only crime was being black.

Despite a statement from a friend who'd survived

    the attack,

And witnesses describing what they'd heard and seen,

The police investigation was biased and flawed,

So justice wasn't served for the murdered teen.

But even though there was abuse from the sceptics,

The Lawrence family refused to accept this.

They challenged the supers, detectives,

The system of law and order's claim to fairness,

Gained awareness.

No spin, just the pain of parents versus the court.

The Macpherson Report

Exposing the truth of institutional racism,

Which many had never given a personal thought.

We owe it to ourselves to work together

For the simple fact we'll share this world forever.

None of us is leaving. If you need something to
    believe in

Let's have unity for Stephen.

Impossible

'Impossible' is a word people use to describe

    something they can't do.

Sometimes they might want to be sadistic,

Call it being 'realistic'

And say it's near enough impossible. 'Nigh' impossible.

They'd like you to think you'll lie in hospital

For defying obstacles and trying not to fall,

But their impossible isn't my impossible.

There are no winners until someone's won it.

You won't know what I'm capable of until I've done it.

I could either stand here patient and listen,

Wanting to make an incision, having to wait for

    permission,

Or I could make a decision, I could take a position.

Impossible is the manifestation of your inhibition,

So fear of trying is fear of flying.

Your mind's racing and your heart isn't out to help,

They're turning against you and you're starting to
doubt yourself.

The nights were cold and the mornings were rough,

Now you're worrying about people calling your bluff,

Second-guessing your ability and all of your stuff,

But no – you alone is more than enough.

This is the truth I saw before I went to sleep:

I knew my time would come eventually,

So I celebrate every test ever sent to me,

Because what's about to be was meant to be.

It's remarkable to try, but I can't afford to die,

Knowing my ambition didn't kill me.

Forget the voice of reason, listen to the real me:

No guts, no glory.

Nothing Left

I give everyone all I've got until there's nothing left

  for her ...

But she doesn't complain cos she's a soldier,

Running the whole show behind the scenes.

She wants appreciation – who needs exposure?

Or is that just what I tell myself, because

Deep down I know she doesn't get enough credit?

Legacy

I can't guarantee that I'll be here in five years

And I'm a man on a mission to share his ideas.

So from time to time, close ones come second

And I have to decline whenever someone beckons

Me over for a laugh and a drink –

That's the nature of my chosen path and I think

It's cos I'm driven by youths in the scariest prisons –

A selfish kind of utilitarianism.

I believe we're stronger than we think.

I believe we can last much longer than we think.

And sociologically I'm a guy that hates differentials,

So nothing bothers me more than wasted potential.

I believe ration can be reconciled with passion

And used to inform whatever style's in fashion.

We tend to get knee-deep in sheer nonsense,

So it's hard to triumph and keep a clear conscience,

And some of us haven't always played the right

positions,

But you're here today because you made the right

decisions.

Congratulations on your success.

I'm sure it was worth all the stress.

Business often gains notoriety

For having no variety and no desire to be

Mindful of its impact on a whole society.

And you could have stayed the same, but you

played the game,

Made respectable objectives and obeyed the aim

Of being fair, through which you made a name.

Business in my community's business in your

community.

Can you honestly say that you're witnessing all

the unity

That there could be? That there should be?

How does one ensure that one's ability

Is geared towards corporate responsibility?

All of the funds, facilities, everyone's fragilities,

All of the workers available to you ...

How can they improve what you pay them all to do

In such a way that benefits everyone who's

    indirectly part of the process?

You render the money and the training all irrelevant

When you don't factor in sustainable development.

Not just to make your corporation more benevolent –

Capitalism is a major force that's prevalent

Globally, true, but locally too.

And driving that force is supposed to be you.

Therefore money can never take the precedence

    that lives do ...

So what drives you?

The aesthetics of human potential?

The feeling you get from perceiving a talent?

Or the accolade of business credentials?

The rewards you receive from achieving a balance?

I haven't said a word you haven't already heard,

But frankly, anyone can learn the lines.

Consider me a polite reminder not to simply

Learn, but to internalise.

You handle yours and I'll mind my own,

That's as fair as this system could ever be.

If we're mindful of the people that we never see

That's the difference between business and legacy.

The Power of Collaboration

Humankind has made so much progress,
And since I want to take part in the glory
It occurs to me that it's a linear process
And I'm part of a story that started before me.
History is the record of decisions we enacted
And that contains knowledge that can't be abstracted.
The excitement of discovery is hard to fathom,
Because there are some feelings you can't imagine,
Like facing a situation as serious as crisis.
And that's why experience is priceless.

Collectively we challenge these forces,
Pool our knowledge and manage resources.
I can't pretend to feel no form of unity
With everyone else in this global community.
We're internationally connected

And this strengthens friendship, as can be expected.

That's why I'm still in touch with my old school teachers;

Humans are essentially social creatures.

We have debates, exacerbate, exaggerate and aggravate,

But make no mistake, we're best when we collaborate.

We'll last longer, no less forever

If we use this life to progress together.

Collaboration has both crowned and killed kings,

It's a way of maximising skill, and skill brings

To life our raw desire to build things,

For innovation and growth or the stimulation of both.

In this climate of global shifts and price inflation

Good ideas don't exist in isolation.

And that's usually apparent

In hotspots for growth opportunity and talent,

But the point is this: the world is expanding;

And even if we gravitate to home,

There's more to explore, but we can't navigate alone.

The future holds unexposed dangers, but no stress –

We're no strangers to progress.

Finance, construction, technology and media:

Trustworthy friends make the journey much easier.

And that's essential to a partnership

Because dialogue is often the harder script to stick

To without too much deviation,

So good friends are due appreciation.

Bear witness and see the intricacy

Of how mutually beneficial good business can be.

Friends save you time and money.

It's an added bonus if you find them funny. ☺

Provided you intend to go the distance,

A good partnership makes loads of difference.

History's a lot like friendship:

It tends to teach us more about ourselves

And helps us lead the march of progress –

In which we can't afford to doubt ourselves.

As we've proven: where collaboration occurs

Progress follows fast.

We dictate what the future holds because

Today's present is tomorrow's past.

All Existence is Contribution

'Knowledge' is a journal of insight.

'Knowledge' is a record of discovery.

You may have had no 'knowledge' of me prior to
this moment,

But I existed before you 'discovered' me.

Knowledge is information that we get to admire.

But what about that which we have yet to acquire?

The bits you neglect, the bits you forget.

Imagine all the knowledge that slips through the net.

Pearls of wisdom that haven't been given that polish;

Understanding you can't access at college,

Simply because it's not accredited according to academia –

It's not knowledge until it's acknowledged.

I believe we have a duty to act on it,

To analyse life and extricate fact from it.

When we take from the world, we don't have to

    subtract from it –

Using what we extract from it, we can impact on it,

Because all existence is contribution.

Ignore the twists and convolution.

There's seven billion people in the world ...

And not one of them has the same fingerprints as you.

Everyone brings something to the table,

But not everyone gets a seat.

And when people don't get a seat,

Then people don't get to eat.

But that's only half of the tragedy.

The other half is equally sad to see.

Remember that knowledge I was talking about?

The one protected by elusion?

Those same people are walking about

With that uncollected contribution.

Untapped potential could be unlocked ability

Hidden wisdom, unsung possibility.

We live in a world that celebrates our young

For being more professional than clever.

As a result, we miss out on a lot of knowledge

At a time when it's more accessible than ever.

'Time' and 'Place' have passed the physical stage;

We now live in the digital age.

And we have much more to contribute

Than unfulfilling jobs for minimal wage.

We want self-determination.

Through self-determination we can help to serve
the nation.

It's not just about success, it's about discovery.

'Growth' means more than economic recovery …

'Growth' is more than earning some paper …

'Growth' is exploring and learning from failure.

Through that process we tend to rise.

And what better teacher than enterprise?

The arena in which ideas centralise

And we truly find out where the potential lies.

It's been a technological world for a long time,

But we're the generation that came of age online.

So there's no way we could all be amateurs.

We form our thoughts in 140 characters.

We share jokes through GIFs and memes

And we've found a brand new home for myths
and dreams.

Progress occurs by many different means.

We owe it to ourselves to listen.

I'm not just the guy that sells the vision.

I'm testament to the fact that with a little help
and wisdom

Young people can be self-sufficient.

Knowledge is information on which we step to
get higher

Into rarefied atmospheres with thin air.

But what about that which we have yet to acquire?

It's not just out there … it's in here.

YOLO

Millions of people in the last six months

Just recently discovered you only live once.

She took hers off, rip yours off,

Now dance on stage until your wig falls off

And ignore the consequences at all costs;

Convince yourself this isn't your loss.

Last time I said YOLO I staggered from the left

    to the right

And I still can't remember the rest of the night.

It's not even a comic, it's a par –

Nathan, I'm sorry for the vomit in your car.

But you know, bro, YOLO.

It's an inefficient reminder

That inhibitions are minor;

Release is a must like a proper safe account,

Cos life's like a calculator and a shotter's amount

    of paper.

At the end of the day, you gotta make it count.

So I live for the moment,

Reassess what I'm prepared to give to the moment,

Allow my focus to shift to the moment,

Symbolised in this drink that I lift to the gift of the

    moment,

Means I'm less likely not to share a detail,

But increase the times I forgot to wear a seatbelt.

See, girls, we males, we could toast to good health,

But we toast to getting one,

And we just say that we're young

And we're supposed to get it wrong,

That's why we get lean as opposed to getting strong,

Then go to the gym and work on our upper-body

    strength,

But we hardly go on treads cos that's cardio and legs.

See we're short-sighted:

We don't know what foresight is.

That's the reason why we laugh wholeheartedly,

And why I don't respect you if you can't go-kart with me.

Nah, don't start with me, you fool.

You blaze a fag,

But since when did you become too cool for Laser Tag?

So you work in an office and your day's a drag –

On the way to the station just race a jag,

Then wipe the sweat from your face and brag

About your new found Jason Statham swag.

That's called YOLO.

But I could lose a brother that fell out with me

And that would bother the hell of out me,

So I'm tearing and calling him up in the prison,

Hearing him falling in love with the vision

Of when he's here and we can ball in another division.

And you hear from me that all of the brothers

    have risen.

I'm repeating myself – no, I keep repeating myself.

All my poems are starting to sound the same,

But it's cool, as long as my heart isn't down the drain.

I wouldn't even mind getting martyred without

    the fame,

Cos you only live once – you gotta make it count.

As much as it's a reason to go mad in the rave,

I'm so glad it's a wave, cos this one makes sense.

It's just used to justify a lot of dumb statements.

I could live my life like a music video,

But those after-effects do stick with me though.

If I use YOLO to help me to sin,

Why wouldn't I use it to help people win?

Especially those with unhealthy beginnings.

Plus if that's the case, you can't tell me a thing.

I might as well be a king,

Cos I could get wasted and buzz about for days,

That says more about me than it does about the phrase.

There's nothing wrong with YOLO,

Even if it starts affecting your health.

All it does is reflect what you expect of yourself.

And this is something not every man likes to say,

But breathing is a luxury and I could die today.

Fam, I would like some change, like a shopkeeper,

So I can't ignore the fact that life's a lot deeper.

Some stuff isn't worth the bull,

Cos some of that dumb stuff's irreversible.

This isn't personal, but I tell myself don't go too crazy,

Cos YOLO could leave you with a whole new baby,

Or if not, the prospect of terminating one,

We find germinating fun, but learning ain't the one.

And some of them STIs can burn and they can bun;

And if I am very loose

And you see me with the pills and the cranberry juice,

You'll be looking at me like I'm actually scum.

So the point is YOLO doesn't have to be dumb.

There's no doubt in my brain that you can change
   the world.

I'd go out of my way to prove it, they can tell,

But if the stake's too high, you gotta take it down,

Cos you only live once, you gotta make it count.

So make it count.

See You on the Other Side

The world is a collection of people's dreams,

Evil schemes and legal teams,

Beautiful children, gleeful teens

In a city full of regal scenes and feeble fiends.

'Market' is the new 'community'.

Hit the right target, you assume impunity.

But at the end of the day, it's you and me.

And whatever it is that's troubling you.

It's not gonna stop us from muddling through.

You can find your answers in the mirror.

One day I'll be in the sky, dancing with Nabila.

One day all of this will go …

But the game is won way before the whistle blows.

Be sure and kiss your foes, life's too short for mistletoes.

You can take this as advice or nothing more than

    wishful prose,

But as long as you take … care.

Take care of yourself when I ain't there.

Take time. Play fair.

There's more to this world than Mayfair.

There's more to this world than there is water in wells.

People like to keep their minds all to themselves,

Try having a thought for someone else for every

    thought of yourself.

Cos there's more to this world.

Spend time finding yourself, spend time with your girl,

Cos time is more precious than diamonds and pearls,

And time flies, but the journey is only ever outbound.

Everything's a countdown.

Think about the past. It's just the bottom half of

    the hourglass.

Sometimes I wonder how we'll last,

But maybe lasting isn't our real task.

So don't be scared, their power's in the fear,

But we have 8,760 hours in the year

And I'd say this whether or not I was in the clear.

Focus on the now, because you're here.

You are exactly where you're supposed to be.

I'm always gonna have you close to me.

Even if we only speak when you go to sleep.

I pray the Lord your soul to keep.

You will always feel love inside

And I'll see you on the other side.

Elephant Knows

I got an offer off a YouTube buzz, cuz.

Non-recoupable one, three hundred grand.

I woulda taken that if it was all about the money,

But they say I'm the one to make the country

    understand …

Make them understand what happens in the ends:

Hood scholar – royals and rappers are my friends.

See I can't forget what I came for,

Can't be a fame-whore.

I don't want slappers and a Benz.

I want higher educational achievement for

    marginalised groups.

I gotta target the right youts.

Consumers on the music market are like shoots:

Deliver that product, you know they'll be back.

That's a platform for me, that's a blessing, a lie?

So I'm stressing at night tryna get the messaging right.

I've gotta show them: you can have a hella good flows

That can translate easily to elegant prose,

But you gotta wake up and smell the Pelican Rouge.

See them ideas? Start developing those

In the time you spend watching all them American
    shows,

Coming out the shower late, swinging your junk,

Checking your phone for women that want to swim
    in your trunks.

Elephant nose. Never forget.

What if I told you *Top Boy* ain't far from the truth?

Would you still turn your nose up and laugh at
    the youth?

What, you don't believe in drugs? I guarantee

You're nothing more than two miles away from a car
    fulla proof.

There's stories to tell. I wanna let my guys pitch in,

But the thought of dry-snitching gets my eyes
    twitching.

One guy's caff is the next guy's kitchen.

Cooking up the food, kids looking up to you.

Feds got you paro, but you ain't shook enough to move

And you wanna be a rapper, but the game's to be sold.

Don't speak on the things you do.

What's the heat gonna bring to you?

What about your connect? Fuck is he gonna think
    of you?

Fam, it's not like you.

Want all them youngers to walk your path,

But someone's gotta talk it darg on your behalf.

Pray you make it if the Lord is willing,

But the world thinks you're just sinning and George
    is winning.

They try dismiss you, simplify this issue:

Either you're the villain or you're chilling.

When the real question is: are you built for the
    struggle?

Or are you comfortable being lazy and helpless?

Cos according to your lady, you're selfless,

But they call you crazy and selfish.

See how fugazi the world is?

Hate the man lives in the Truth,

But they love-off the one telling them fibs in

    the booth.

Walking contradictions. Celibate hoes,

But no jealousy for anybody selling their souls.

We only 'cheque' for reality – hell of a dose …

Cos what's the point in selling them o's

If you ain't using that power to benefit those

From a place where money does grow on trees,

But the government cuts it off whenever it grows.

We never get loads.

I'd call them Pinocchios, but the blow's

Left them with an elephant nose.

Never forget.

An elephant knows to never forget.

Acknowledgements

Some of the most important facts of my life were completely beyond my control, yet all seemed to work in my favour. For this reason, I thank God and I thank my ancestors. I honour my parents for not only bringing me into this world, but also for providing me with the tools to build in a land foreign to them. Looking sensible now, aren't we? Thanks to Freddie, Nanteza, Nnakku, Michael and Kenny for loving honestly and keeping me grounded. Special regards to Coach Junior – I wish everyone had one of you. Although I'm deeply grateful to all my friends, a special thanks goes to Damini, Nathan, Kalil, Fahad, Suuna and Sandra, love you guys. God bless my partners in crime, B and D (from Sunday!). I'll always give it up for my birthplace, north-west London, but my heart still remains with my fam in Uganda. I'd also like to thank Zeon and Wretch for stepping up to the plate. Thanks to Ebury, Random House, Island Records and, most importantly, all my supporters – it's for you.